Those Magnificent Trains

Those Magnificent Trains

An American Anthology

BY CHARLES E. DITLEFSEN

CEDCO

Cedco Publishing Company

San Rafael, California

First Edition

This book published by Cedco Publishing
Company, 2955 Kerner Blvd., San Rafael,
CA 94901

Printed in Korea

ISBN 1-55912-153-X

Three Union Pacific steam engines hibernate during the winter of 1977 in the Cheyenne, Wyoming, roundhouse.

Those Magnificent Trains®

An American Anthology

BY CHARLES E. DITLEFSEN

One of the Pennsylvania Railroad's famous K4-type Pacific 4-6-2 locomotives speeds a commute train through Red Bank, New Jersey, in 1953.

CONTENTS

INTRODUCTION

There is something about trains that speaks of romance to me. I think it is something similar to the romantic notions that surround legends of cowboys, something of a grand and glorious time that is now mostly past. The developing years of the railroads are almost coincident with the nineteenth century, while the twentieth century has seen their maturation and decline.

The thrust of this work is to capture some of the feel that trains evoke, through the use of color photography. To those who have a knowledge of the subject, I hope this photographic sojourn will bring some added insight and feel for the romance of railroading. And, for those who are new to an interest in trains, I hope this work brings enjoyment and a broadened horizon. □

The westbound Rio Grande Zephyr approaches tunnel #29 near Pinecliffe, Colorado, some thirty-seven miles west of Denver in 1979.

Milwaukee Road electric box motor #E34 is crossing the viaduct at Penfield, Montana, in 1964.

For Jeanette...

Those Magnificent Trains

A LOOK AT AMERICAN RAILROADING

At this point in history there are still ten major railroads in America and numerous minor and short-line railroads. Railroads today still carry over 35 percent of all the intercity freight traffic in the U.S. and Canada. However, in terms of percentages, the passenger traffic on today's railroads is very, very small.

Today's modern railroad bears little resemblance to the railroads of a hundred years ago. All but gone are the passenger trains that once carried all of the intercity traffic in America. Gone is the Pullman Company which once operated a rolling hotel that had two hundred thousand beds to offer all over this land. Gone are the steam locomotives that have captured the hearts of so many of us in this latter half of the twentieth century. Gone are the tens of thousands of small train stations that at one time were found in any small burg you could think of. Long gone is the idea of railroads as the most important industry in America. Railroads today are lean, trim, hard-working machines that have to compete with airplanes, cars, trucks, and a host of other things unknown a hundred years ago.

While we will be taking a passing look at the trains and railroads of today, in this work the real focus will be in the glory days of the past which are now available to us only in historical accounts, photographic records, and a few railroad museums scattered across the land.

The idea of steel wheels on steel rails was first developed in England in the late eighteenth century. Horses pulled cars of ore at coal mines. The invention of the steam engine and the tubular boiler, by George Stephenson, led to the

A mixture of ultra-modern Southern Pacific and Rio Grande power pose for the photographer at the Roseville, California, yard in 1989.

Motive power of the Cotton Belt and the Union Pacific are combined on this freight train heading west across the Sierra Nevada, near Cisco, California.

An eastbound Chessie System coal train fills the New River Gorge with the sound of EMD turbochargers as it works uphill through Thurmond, West Virginia.

development of the "modern" steam engine of the last century. The Baltimore and Ohio was the first railroad in America. Chartered in 1827 and opened in 1830, it experimented with horses and even sails before steam was adopted as the best source of power.

Railroad development in the the United States had to adapt itself to the needs of a new and rapidly growing country, a large part of which was first made available for settlement by the railroads. In 1830 there were thirty miles of railroad in operation in the United States. By 1847 there were 5,206 miles and by 1860, over twenty thousand miles.

The Civil War brought railroad development to a grinding halt. But, after the war was over, the railroads really took off. The year 1869 saw the opening of the first transcontinental rail link. It was now possible to travel from New York to San Francisco in as little as one week. This was a vast improvement over the three- or four-month trek by wagon train or the very treacherous journey by sea around Cape Horn.

At their peak in about 1920 American railroads operated about two hundred thousand miles of track and offered both freight and passenger service almost everywhere. At this time railroads accounted for almost all of the intercity freight and passenger business in the United States and Canada, and, in terms of their business success, showered net earnings of almost 10 percent of their net worth year after year.

The automobile and the truck started to make serious inroads against the railroads in the 1920s, and that is when the railroads started to shrink. The Great Depression did not help the railroads at all. The progress of highways for automobiles and trucks and the development of the airplane forced the

Southern Pacific 4-6-2 #2476 speeds a northbound commute train through Burlingame on its way to San Francisco in 1955.

railroads to start cutting back.

The Second World War with its tremendous industrial need brought the railroads back to life for a while, but, after the war was over, the writing was on the wall for the future of the railroads.

The 1960s, 1970s, and 1980s saw one merger after another and one abandonment after another.

The basic principle of the steel wheel on the steel rail seems to be sound, and the recognition of the energy efficiency inherent in this principle may be turning things around once again as we reach the end of this century. There is also the question of the real limits of energy available to us. Those factors may combine to bring us more railroads in the next century, not less. Already we are seeing a strong move to more passenger commuter lines in one city after another in the United States.

What the future holds may be very bright for those of us who hold trains and railroads in high regard. □

Baltimore & Ohio's #6119, a 2-10-2, heads a westbound freight up Sand Patch Grade at Manila, Pennsylvania, in 1956.

Denver & Rio Grande Western freight #138 is passing the Crystal Lakes near Leadville, Colorado, in 1986.
The highest peak in the background is Mt. Massive, the second highest peak in Colorado.

A spectacular sunset finds Burlington Northern's eastbound freight #170 in a siding along the Columbia River at McCredie, Washington. The lead unit, #2713, is a GP 38-2.

25

Smoking up a storm, two Union Pacific 4-8-4s, #827 and #838, speed westbound mail train #27 near Borie, Wyoming, in 1955.

A Southern Pacific rotary snowplow works westbound through Yuba Pass in the unusually sunny weather of December 1982.

A STORY OF
STEAM AND DIESEL

No one today will argue whether the railroads should operate with steam engines or diesel engines. However, that was not always the case. The steam engine was first developed for use on the railroads in the 1820s in England. Three steam engines were imported to America in 1829, and the first trial run was held on August 8, 1829, at Honesdale, Pennsylvania.

From that time, up until the last steam engine was built in America by the Norfolk & Western in 1950, the technology developed to an amazing degree. New steam engines are still being built in China today because of the abundance of coal and cheap labor and an acute shortage of diesel fuel.

The revolution brought about by the steam engine as a means of transportation can best be measured by contrast with the methods it superseded. Prior to the development of the steam engine, a system of transportation by stage coaches and heavier vehicles flourished and was supported by highway systems that were continuously improved. Maximum speeds of up to eight, ten and twelve miles per hour were possible by stage coach on these highways. For a journey from New York to Washington, D.C., outside passengers were charged twenty dollars and inside passengers, thirty dollars. The entire trip took forty hours. By the turn of the century the same journey could be made in about eight hours and cost between seven and eight dollars. Today the journey costs about thirty dollars and takes only three hours on Amtrak's high-speed electric trains which attain speeds of over 120 miles per hour.

Four Boston & Maine steam engines are steamed up and ready for service at the Reading Highlands, Massachusetts, roundhouse in 1953.

The first steam locomotive, built by Baldwin Locomotive Works of Philadelphia, was advertised to pull thirty tons on level track but was not to be operated on rainy days. By 1900 Baldwin was turning out locomotives that would pull five thousand tons on the level, and by 1941 engines like the Union Pacific "Big Boy" would pull over ten thousand tons.

The diesel locomotive was invented by a German by the name of Rudolph Diesel in 1898, and its application to railroads was quickly envisioned.

The Chicago, Burlington & Quincy Railroad operated the first main line diesel locomotive on a railroad on its Zephyr high-speed passenger service between Chicago and Denver in 1934. The application of the diesel engine to railroading was seen as an immediate success by many railroaders, but not all.

By the 1940s the steam engine had been refined to a high degree. It took ten to fifteen years for the diesel to catch up to the steam engine. There were certain favorable factors, however, about the diesel's operation that no one could deny. For one thing, they did not require large amounts of water to operate. The basic principle of the steam engine is that you have a fire and a boiler which takes a large amount of water, boils the water into steam, and pressurizes the steam that makes the engine go.

Out on the deserts of the West, the steam engines required a lot of water, and it was always a problem for the railroads to provide that water. The diesel locomotive solved the problem of large water use because it used almost none.

As labor became an expensive factor in the 1940s, the diesel locomotive provided another advantage in that many locomotives could operate together with just one engineer and one fireman. When steam engines operate together, each engine must have an engineer and a fireman. Put three steam engines together, and you need three engineers and three firemen. If you put six diesels together, you still need only one engineer and one fireman. And, to put the icing on the cake, it turned out that the diesel engine was much easier and less costly to maintain than the old steam engine. So, by the time twenty years had passed since the first diesel was introduced on the railroads, diesel had almost totally supplanted steam.

Steam engines, howerever, were more interesting to look at and carried much more emotional appeal than did the diesels. When I was growing up, I can remember railfans talking about how they just hated diesels—because they were not as "neat" as steam engines. In any event, by 1960 there were virtually no steam engines running on any major railroads in America. Many, however, were saved in parks and by various railroad historical groups. Because steam engines are so "neat," many groups have endeavored to bring back to life their favorite steam engine that had been saved in a park somewhere. And, they have been uncannily successful at this.

One of the most famous examples is the restoration of ex-Southern Pacific #4449 from a park in Portland. The locomotive had been donated to the City of Portland by the Southern Pacific in the 1950s, and was displayed by the city in a park. This was the only class 4400 SP locomotive saved. This particular class of steam engine was considered by many to be the most beautiful locomotive ever built.

In 1973, with the American bicentennial fast approaching, there was much

talk of putting together an American Freedom Train that would run around the country and display many of our nation's historical documents, such as the Constitution and the Declaration of Independence. A locomotive needed to be selected to pull this train. A group or private businessmen donated $1 million to pay for the restoration of #4449 to operating condition, so it could do the honors at the head of the American Freedom Train. This was but the beginning of what has become a mass restoration of old steam locomotives in America. Personally, I can't even keep up with all the steam engines that are being put back into service. In the 1980s, the Norfolk Southern had a whole department set up just to restore and maintain their old steam engines. The Union Pacific Railroad donated materials, supplies, and facilities for the restoration of their 4-6-6-4 "Challenger" #3985. Union Pacific employees donated their time to put this engine back into operating condition. Although this process took years, it was a labor of love.

While the steam engine will never again be an economical source of power for American railroads, there are more of them running now than there have been in the past thirty years. Also, there is every indication that more are on their way back to operating condition.

Norfolk & Western #605, a 4-8-4 "J" class locomotive, is on the head end of train #8 near Montvale, Virginia, in 1957.

There is nothing in the world like standing alongside the tracks and watching a steam engine go by at a thunderous speed; or riding behind a steam engine with a heavy load as it works up a grade, wondering if it will make it; or catching the gleam in a young child's eye as he watches this monster of steam, fire, and steel roar down the track. □

Union Pacific steam locomotive #3985, a 4-6-6-4 Challenger, is at the Cheyenne, Wyoming, roundhouse in 1982. This engine was rebuilt in 1980-81 by volunteers with the help of the Union Pacific Railroad, and it is operated for special occasions.

Ex-Southern Pacific #4449, a 4-8-4, is northbound with Mt. Shasta in the background in 1981.

The #4449 is in its American Freedom Train colors as it speeds northbound along the Santa Fe mail line between San Diego and San Juan Capistrano in 1976.

Looking like the Pennsylvania's Buffalo Express, PRR E8 #5898 leads an excursion train on the Blue Mountain and Reading Railroad at Glen, Pennsylvania, in 1987.

Deep in the Sacramento River Canyon south of Dunsmuir, California, a northbound Southern Pacific freight, powered by a Cab-forward 4-8-8-2 and a 2-8-2 helper, #3300, holds in a siding as a diesel-powered freight passes. The year was 1951.

A LITTLE NOSTALGIA

I grew up in the declining days of railroading, in the 1950s. My father was a railfan, and he passed his hobby on to me at a very young age. When I was a young boy, I used to go off with him on many journeys to watch trains around Los Angeles where we lived. We lived within two blocks of the Huntington Drive line of the Pacific Electric, and, though I was only three years old, I can still remember passing those old interurbans at night along Huntington Drive, their step lights glowing in the dark, sparks occasionally coming from where their trolley pole met the overhead wire.

I remember going to the Southern Pacific station in Glendale to watch the "Coast Daylight" depart for the last time behind steam. It was 1955. To a seven-year-old boy those 4400s of the Southern Pacific were huge machines, virtually alive, as they hissed and smoked and steamed and dripped.

Most opportunities I had to see steam engines were on various fan trips that were operated in the Los Angeles area. The only difference between the steam fan trips of the 1950s and the steam fan trips of today was then most people thought that would be the last time steam would ever run on that particular line.

The fear that the steam engine might break down was as common in the 1950s as it is today. I can recall one fan trip back in the mid-fifties behind two 4400s on the Southern Pacific from Los Angeles to Bakersfield and return. We had a photo stop at Caliente Curve on the way back, and the booster motor on one of the engines failed. They couldn't get the train started again up the hill. We waited for what seemed hours as it started to snow. Finally a six-unit set of

The Pacific Electric Railway was once the largest interurban railway in the world, spanning much of California with over two thousand miles of track. This P.E. "Blimp" #1540 is about to leave L.A.'s Main Street Station a few days before the line was abandoned in 1961.

blue Santa Fe FTs showed up and hooked onto the front of our train. Off we went like that all the way to Los Angeles.

There was another fan trip to Bakersfield with a cab-forward and a 4400 with a photo stop at Tehachapi Loop. The train backed around the loop for a photo runby. I sat on the lap of the engineer of the 4400 as we went both ways around the loop. I was six or seven at the time. And, people ask me why I began to love trains at such an early age! ☐

A perfectly matched set of Santa Fe FTs drag a westbound freight near Bealville, California, on Southern Pacific's Mojave-Bakersfield main line over which the Santa Fe maintains operating rights giving them access to Northern California.

Great Northern electric #5019 is at Skykomish, Washington, in 1955. These locomotives were the "Big Boys" of electric power in the United States. Great Northern had only two of them. They were General Electric class W-1.

Chicago, Burlington & Quincy's "E" unit #9948-A is on the point of train #27 westbound at Council Bluffs, Iowa, in 1958.

A Southern Pacific class 4400, 4-8-4, heads the southbound train #20, the "Klamath Express," a mail and express train. This scene is typical of SP's mountain railroading north of Redding in the days of steam operations.

Grand Trunk Western's #6408, a 4-8-4, speeds eastbound with train #22, at Bloomfield Hills, Michigan, in 1958.

A Union Pacific hot shop piggyback train, headed by DDA40X "Centennial"-type locomotive #6942, roars eastbound up the 2.2 percent grade of Cajon Pass in Southern California in 1978.

Two of Norfolk Southern's massive C39-8s lead a coal train southbound at Frisco, Tennessee. The train was loaded at Appalachia, Virginia, and was headed for a power plant in Georgia. The year was 1987.

49

Sierra Railway's #3, a 4-4-0 "American"-type locomotive, puts on a show of steam and smoke for photographers at Jamestown, California, in 1969. The Sierra Railway has been a favorite of movie studios. In 1921 The Traveling Salesman was shot on the Sierra. In more recent years the TV series "Petticoat Junction" and "Death Valley Days" were filmed there.

Colorado & Southern #806, a 2-8-2, is on a southbound sugar beet train doing some street running in Ft. Collins, Colorado, in 1957.

PASSENGER TRAINS

The nice thing about passenger trains is that you can ride on them. All over America people did ride on them. At one time passenger trains connected every city and town in this great land of ours. Before the age of the automobile and the airplane there really wasn't any other way to get around, except on horseback or by stagecoach. At the turn of the last century 99 percent of all intercity passenger traffic was accounted for by the railroads. Today that number is less then one-tenth of 1 percent. People were riding trains from their very inception. In fact, going for a train ride was something of a fad in the early to mid-nineteenth century.

Passenger trains were not much more than boxcars with benches until after the Civil War when George Mortimer Pullman, an American inventor, developed the Pullman palace car. This car was a sleeping car with very comfortable beds. It was a hotel on rails. The Pullman Palace Car Company was founded in 1867 and by the 1920s was effectively the largest hotel chain in the world with some ten thousand cars and over two hundred thousand beds in operation every night.

Santa Fe's Grand Canyon is westbound at Cajon Summit with F3 #19 leading a set of five "F" units. These "F" units were capable of speeds up to 120 miles per hour and were often clocked at these speeds on long straight-aways in California, Arizona, and New Mexico in the 1950s and early 1960s.

The development of the diesel locomotive in the 1930s was soon followed by the emergence of the sleek, streamlined passenger trains that flourished in the 1940s and 1950s. Names like "Twentieth Century Limited," "Broadway Limited," "Super Chief," and "California Zephyr" conjure up memories of a time when traveling by train was the only way to go. These trains offered meal service that could rival some of the best restaurants. Long before the days of microwave ovens and frozen foods, fresh food was cooked on the trains in the dining cars, and the service was impeccable.

From a purely economic perspective the passenger trains were never very successful. What finally stopped the passenger trains was a seemingly unrelated event. In 1966 the United States Post Office introduced the zip code system. Until that time the railroad carried all of the first-class mail on their passenger trains. If you wanted your mail to go air-mail, you had to pay twice the first-class rate. The zip code system changed all that; now all first-class mail would go by air.

Chicago, Burlington & Quincy's Denver Zephyr in the charge of four "E" units is being serviced at Burlington, Iowa, in 1968.

Within days of that decision, virtually all the railroads petitioned the Interstate Commerce Commission for permission to abandon their passenger service. By 1970 there were only a handful of passenger trains still running in this country. Then, in the baseless hope that passenger trains could survive with the support of the federal government, Congress created Amtrak. Laden with controversy from its inception, Amtrak has not provided even a shadow of the passenger service that once was.

55

Denver & Rio Grande Western's Ski Train is just coming off of the wye at Tabernash after having been turned and is headed back to Winter Park. On Saturdays and Sundays during the ski season the Rio Grande operates this ski train between Denver and Winter Park. Often a railroad executive's business car can be found at the rear of the train.

56

Western Pacific's eastbound California Zephyr glides through the Feather River Canyon near Pulga, California, behind three of the WP's "F" units. The California Zephyr connected San Francisco with Chicago and operated over three railroads: the Western Pacific, the Rio Grande, and the Chicago, Burlington & Quincy. It was considered by many to be one of the best rides in America.

An almost-forgotten fact about passenger trains is that they are very fuel efficient — about one hundred times more efficient than an airplane. That being the case, and with the escalating cost of energy, we could see the rebirth of the passenger train as a viable and economical form of transportation in the not-too-distant future. □

Norfolk & Western's #611, a 4-8-4 class "J," is hauling the 1986 edition of the "Independence Limited" westbound across Big Four Creek at Big Four, West Virginia.

New York Central's #4002 leads another "E" unit eastbound out of the maze of trackage that is Chicago in 1958.

Chicago & Eastern Illinois' #1609, an FP7, leads a three-car local out of Chicago in 1956. In the background is Dearborn Station which was once used by the Santa Fe, the Erie, and the C&EI as well as several other railroads. It is now long gone.

Canadian National Railway's #5702, a 4-6-4, is on passenger train #80 east of Bay View, Ontario, in 1958.

Norfolk & Western steam engines #611, a 4-8-4, and #1218, a 2-6-6-4, pace each other up the Christinburg, Virginia, grade at Elliston, Virginia, in 1987. This event was for the benefit of the National Railway Historical Society's 1987 convention which was held in Roanoke, Virginia.

In the late 1940s and early 1950s General Motors' E7s were standard power for Southern Pacific's Sunset Limited and Golden State Limited passenger trains. Here we see two sets of this power being serviced at Taylor Yard, the SP's major facility in Los Angeles.

The addition of a third San Joaquin Valley passenger train to the Oakland-Bakersfield service in 1989 prompted the making of this symbolic promotional picture of three Amtrak units at night for the cover of the Amtrak California Timetable. The photograph was made at the West Oakland Amtrak facility with the help of friendly switching crews and a small smoke generator.

A big Arizona moon rises over the Santa Fe branch line at Ash Fork, where the power for tomorrow's Clarkdale turn rests in the yard.

Great Western Railway's #90, a 2-10-0, is seen here rolling a sugar beet rain across Roulard Lake in Northern Colorado in 1961. No. 90 was later sold to the Strasburg Railway in Pennsylvania, where it is still in operable condition.

All the familiar views of distant trains climbing the canyons of the Feather River Canyon are lost to sight in the falling snow of a Sierra Nevada blizzard which limits our vision to objects nearby. At Keddie Wye we see very little beyond a red signal protecting the twin rails of the Northern California Extension as they diverge through a tunnel toward a meeting with those of the Burlington Northern at Bieber, south of Klamath Falls.

A Southern Pacific Spreader plows snow at speed, working west through Emigrant Gap, California. This spreader will work a few miles west up to a balloon track where it will turn and head back east.

Under heavy rains a contingent of General Motors' finest speeds a Santa Fe freight across the Martian landscape of the Mojave Desert near Bagdad, California.

*From up on Bolo Hill east of Amboy we look across the Mojave Desert
at the doubletrack Santa Fe main line, glimpsing the distant, dusty
meeting of high-speed freight trains as they race toward opposite coasts.
Soon the dots of colored light are all that will be left behind the departing
trains: signal talk repeating visual chants of green, yellow and red.*

71

Chessie System F7s power a passenger special past the storefronts of the former mining and railroad town of Thurmond, West Virginia, in 1989.

Throughout the winter of 1987, the worst winter in nearly fifty years, Norfolk Southern was able to keep its trains rolling. As the clouds gave way to the winter sun, southbound train #127, headed by a N&W SD 40-2, splits a signal at Ruffin, North Carolina, in a very rare twenty inches of snow.

NORTH OF THE BORDER

While all of the preceding was going on in the United States, the economics of the industry were working in a very similar manner in Canada.

The late nineteenth century saw the development of two transcontinental railroads: the Canadian Pacific and the Canadian National. The Canadian Pacific was owned by private industry; the Canadian National was owned by the government. Both railroads operated from Toronto/Montreal, across the vast reaches of the Canadian prairies, to Vancouver.

Some of the most spectacular scenery to be found in North America is in Canada, to which the photographs on these pages attest.

The history of passenger trains in Canada is very similar to that of the United States. VIA, Canada's version of Amtrak, was formed in the early 1970s. VIA promised the people of Canada it would carry on the fine passenger service offered by the railroads up until that time. However, government promises being what they are, most of the VIA trains were discontinued in early 1990, because the government didn't want to spend the money to support this mode of transportation.

In 1977 British Columbia Railway sent its Royal Hudson #2860, a 4-6-4, on a goodwill tour of the lower forty-eight states. The purpose of this expedition was to promote tourism in British Columbia. In this scene we see the Hudson as it passes the station at Saugus, northbound on Southern Pacific's Los Angeles-San Francisco Coast Line.

In addition to the two major transcontinental railroads, numerous smaller railroads have flourished in Canada. The British Columbia Railway which runs from Vancouver north to Prince Ruppert and the Algoma Central Railway which operates in Ontario are two that come to mind. □

A Canadian Pacific freight winds its way around the Lower Spiral Tunnel of CPR's trans-continental line through the Canadian Rockies. The caboose at the far left of the photograph is the end of the train.

Deep in the Fraser River Canyon at Cisco, British Columbia, two widebody SD 50s take flight over the Fraser River late on an August 1989 afternoon. Darkness will fill the canyon before this westbound train reaches its destination of Vancouver.

Two MLW (Montreal Locomotive Works) M630s lead southbound train #14 toward Vancouver at Britannia Beach, BC, on the British Columbia Railway's main line.

COLORADO
NARROW GAUGE

Dear to the hearts of most railroad enthusiasts are the narrow-gauge railroads that once flourished in Colorado. Narrow gauge refers to the spacing between the two rails. On standard-gauge railroads, which virtually all railroads are today, the rails are laid 4 feet 8½ inches apart. On the narrow-gauge lines of Colorado the rails are three feet apart. Reasons for this were that the trains could negotiate much sharper curves, could go up steeper grades, and cost much less to build. Because of the rugged terrain in Colorado, these little narrow-gauge railroads were much more practical when it came to reaching remote mining communities such as Durango, Silverton, Telluride, or Ridgeway. Numerous narrow-gauge lines were built in Colorado, the Denver & Rio Grande being the biggest and best known as well as the longest lasting.

The Rio Grande Southern, which connected Durango with Telluride and Ridgeway, was well known and admired because of its collection of unusual rolling stock. Known as the "Galloping Geese," these railcars had gasoline engines and were constructed from old motor cars. Although they had the appearance of a homemade bus or truck, they cost very little to operate and allowed the railroad to continue operation into the 1950s.

Other lines such as the giant Colorado & Southern and the tiny Silverton Northern all had their day in the great era of narrow-gauge railroading in Colorado. Of this once vast network, only the Durango & Silverton Railroad and the Cumbres & Toltec Scenic Railroad remain today.

The Durango & Silverton operates on the old route of the Denver & Rio

Denver & Rio Grande Western's narrow-gauge K-28-class engine #476 is kept with a full head of steam and ready for service at the Durango, Colorado, roundhouse in the summer of 1968.

Grande Western between Durango and Silverton in Southern Colorado. This railroad principally carries tourists up the Animas River Canyon to Silverton. It is undoubtedly one of the most scenically spectacular railroad trips in the world.

The Cumbres & Toltec Scenic Railroad is also principally a tourist line and operates between Chama, New Mexico, and Antinito, Colorado. It too is on an old section of the Denver & Rio Grande Western, but, due to its remoteness, it does not draw nearly as much business as the Durango & Silverton.

Because of their small size, the engines and trains of the narrow-gauge railroads hold a certain charm. They represent an event in human history that is truly unique. □

D&RGW engines #483, a K-36, and #473, a K-28, are stopped for water and servicing at Sublett, New Mexico. This was the last narrow-gauge train to run from Alamosa to Durango. The date was December 5, 1968.

Photo Credits:

With #484 on the point and #480 pushing, these two K-36s of the D&RGW take eight boxcars from Cumbres to Chama in 1963.

D&RGW #498, a K-37, takes an eastbound narrow-gauge train across Gato Trestle, a few miles east of Chama, New Mexico, in the summer of 1967.

Union Pacific's rebuilt Challenger 4-6-6-4 #3985 blasts northbound from Salt Lake City to Ogden near Kaysville, Utah, in 1982.

Milwaukee Road's Box Cab #E-39 has just coupled onto its freight train and is getting ready to head west from Othello, Washington, to Tacoma in 1964.